# BROKEN WARRIOR

Be Empowered to Overcome

Marteka Landrum

Springdale, Arkansas

Copyright © 2021 Marteka Landrum

All rights reserved. No part of this book may be reproduced or used in any manner of media or otherwise without written permission by the copyright owner except for the use of quotations in a book review.

ISBN: 978-1-7369694-0-3 (paperback)
ISBN: 978-1-7369694-1-0 (Ebook)
ISBN: 978-1-7369694-2-7 (Audiobook)
ISBN: 978-1-7369694-3-4 (Marshallese)
ISBN: 978-1-7369694-4-1 (Spanish)
ISBN: 978-1-7369694-5-1 (Swahilli)

Publisher's Cataloging-In-Publication Data
(Prepared by The Donohue Group, Inc.)

Names: Landrum, Marteka, author.
Title: Broken warrior : be empowered to overcome / Marteka Landrum.
Description: Springdale, Arkansas : Positive Changes 11, [2021]
Identifiers: ISBN 9781736969403 (paperback) | ISBN 9781736969410 (ePub)
Subjects: LCSH: Self-actualization (Psychology)--Religious aspects--Christianity. | Fortitude--Religious aspects--Christianity. | Resilience (Personality trait)--Religious aspects--Christianity. | Psychic trauma--Religious aspects--Christianity.
Classification: LCC BV4598.2 .L36 2021 (print) | LCC BV4598.2 (ebook) | DDC 248.4--dc23

Library of Congress Control Number: 2021913521

Scripture quotations marked KJV are from the King James Version of the Bible. The KJV is public domain in the United States. Scripture quotations marked NLT are from the Holy Bible, New Living Translation, copyright © 1996, 2004, 2015 by Tyndale House Foundation. Used by permission of Tyndale House Publishers, Inc., Carol Stream, Illinois 60188. All rights reserved. Scripture quotations marked ESV are from the English Standard Version The Holy Bible, English Standard Version. ESV® Text Edition: 2016. Copyright © 2001 by Crossway Bibles, a publishing ministry of Good News Publishers. Scripture quotations marked NKJV are taken from the New King James Version®. Copyright © 1982 by Thomas Nelson. Used by permission. All rights reserved. Scripture quotations marked NIV are from the Holy Bible, New International Version®, NIV® Copyright ©1973, 1978, 1984, 2011 by Biblica, Inc.® Used by permission. All rights reserved worldwide. Scripture quotations marked GNT are from the Good News Translation, Copyright © 1992 by American Bible Society. Scripture quotations marked TPT are from The Passion Translation®. Copyright © 2017 by BroadStreet Publishing© Group, LLC . Used by permission. All rights reserved. thePassionTranslation.com

Positive Changes 11 LLC 2811 Springdale Ave. #7442 Springdale, AR 72764

Book Cover: Klressa Barnes
Interior Design: Kavidha Rajavelu

# DEDICATION

*To those who are searching for their identity, place, voice, or any combination of those. Your past does not define you. Keep pressing in until you break through and then launch out. I see you.*

# TABLE OF CONTENTS

*Dedication*     *iii*
*Acknowledgments*     *vii*
*Foreword*     *ix*
*Preface*     *xi*
*Prologue*     *xiii*
*Introduction*     *xv*

**Deal with the Lies**     1

**Get Out of the Box**     15

**Determine that Obedience is Better Than Comfort**     21

**Recognize Who Abba Created You to Be**     27

**Learn to Accept Freedom**     33

*Conclusion*     *41*
*Resources*     *45*
*About the Author*     *49*

# ACKNOWLEDGMENTS

Special thanks to those who supported this book:

- Clarice Dailey
- Mary Scott
- Sue Joachims
- London Sanitago
- Carla Breckenridge
- Margie Lillig
- Sharene Urban
- Beth Winger
- Angie Brown
- Laura Sossamon
- Cecil Washington, Jr.
- Jeanne Haraldson
- Jeanette Wilson
- LaTonya Jackson
- LaTroya Sampson
- Daniel McGee
- Gloria Davis
- Alicia Landrum
- Stevetta Dickerson
- Anica Thompson
- Jimmy McGee
- Magdalena Terrell
- Dennis Petersen
- Kimberly Nelson
- Sherilyn Tauber
- Kimberly Bishop
- Brandon Landrum
- Nancy Guest
- Patrick Ramsey
- Elaine Couch
- David Harder
- Sarah Walden
- Cynthia Smart
- Sandy Harder
- Lois Johnson
- Thelma Landrum
- Evelyn Jones
- Alesia Arnold
- Justin Mills
- Donald Johnston
- Sharon Urban
- Priscilla Samson
- Angela Gatewood
- Andria Ginyard
- Tamra Turrentine
- Kathy Garland
- Sheryl Landon
- Doris Pyles

- Emily Pilcher
- Deborah Landrum
- Anita Spires
- Rose Shively
- Marilyn Williams
- Kay Beauchesne
- The Rock of Northwest Arkansas
- Rebbecca Shipman
- Brittany Birch
- Renee Jones
- Lesia Carter
- Emma Wilson
- Becky Wong
- Peggy Elliott Pugh

# FOREWORD

Since the fall of man, people have been on a quest to find peace. While many choose to turn to human wisdom, which can only give temporary or numbing relief, some have chosen to turn to their loving heavenly Father, Abba, to find true and eternal comfort.

Marteka's honesty and rawness throughout "Broken Warrior" allows the reader to not only peek into the depth of pain and anguish she endured, but more importantly her awakening to an overcoming relationship with Abba. Just like the rebirth Yahshua described to Nicodemus, a teacher of Israel, Marteka walks you down the path of revelation of your personal identity in Christ apart from your past and fears.

No matter your journey, the Father has an answer for your past, present and future. For those who trust Him, He will never leave you in a state less than what He intended from the beginning. His heart for you is to be whole!! Shalom, which in Hebrew means peace, wholeness, safety, completeness, prosperity, welfare and tranquility, is a state of being which only Yahweh can provide through His Son Yahshua.

I know you will be blessed and changed as you walk with Holy Spirit through the pages of this book. The Father's heart is for you to be whole and Marteka's words will inspire and direct your path all along the way.

Enjoy.

Autumn Murner

Daughter and Minister of the One True God, Yahweh

# PREFACE

Although this book has been in process for several years, it finally began to take shape in the summer of 2020. At the beginning of the year, the Lord told me it was time for my voice to be heard. I became intentional in writing my story. I saw a self-publishing course advertised. The Lord gave the green light and I enrolled in this six-week course. It turned into a writing course since none of us had completed a manuscript. I did not have an audience or purpose statement at the time. All I knew was that I was to write. My story was painful, but the Lord had already told me that it had to be shared. I did not fight His request or the process. I was encouraged to just write. So I did. Yet again writing has proven to be very healing for me.

I knew that I wanted people to be free. I did not want to focus on the bad things that happened. One day in July, my writing coach gave me an assignment on forgiveness. I wrote five letters: offender, my five-year-old self, both of my parents, and me now. I wrote without thinking about it, forgave, and released each person to go live their best life now.

Forgiveness comes in layers. That day in July was a deeper level of forgiveness for a traumatic event. Now I saw how the lies I had believed because of this event affected every area of my life. The directions after writing were to wait two hours, read them out loud, call each one "ashes," put them in a bucket, and set them on fire. I had no idea how freeing that would be! Yes, it did set off the smoke alarm. It also made way for the next turning point at the end of that month.

The forgiveness exercise and the ministry time gave me the tools to get rid of all the junk that was blocking me from being who Abba created me to be. Now that I could see and hear without all the interference, things began to click: audience, purpose, revised outline. Yes, this book is about trauma; however, the focus is on FREEDOM.

# PROLOGUE

This book is evidence of a faithful Creator. I decided to trust Him with every fiber of my being. He turned everything around to work out for my good. Writing this book gave me the opportunity to "face the music." For so long I had been trying to avoid pain in one area all the while aggravating it in several other areas. I was good at hiding. Making the conscious decision to stop hiding and come to the front of the room has been life changing. Everything that was holding me back is gone. I am free to be who I was created to be. Freedom is such an amazing feeling. Every obstacle was worth it. I had a huge paradigm shift. Not only am I happy, but I also now have joy. I know my position. I know how to operate from there. Everything is clear now. Abba is the pilot. I choose to trust Him. I am the passenger. I love the view from up here.

# INTRODUCTION

When trauma occurs, it creates a rift that affects every area in your life. It is interesting how trauma affects people. Some go numb, some bury it, and others act out. Even in acting out, it can look so many different ways, which is why counseling is so necessary. Some cultures maintain a negative view of counseling. There are times when we need to talk with trained professionals to help us sort out our emotions, behaviors, and thoughts. Some people prefer to seek counseling with the leaders of their faith community. Either way, the counselor is there to listen objectively and ask questions. There will be times when they explain what you have shared. In my personal experience, there were times when I left the session exhausted from the deep emotional work that had just taken place. Despite this, I felt better. Better yet, I felt free from the effects of trauma—and so can you.

A person must know how to communicate their emotions. Everyone was born knowing how to feel. God gave us emotions because He wants us to be expressive. As we grow, adults teach us about emotions through their actions. These actions shape us. Their words have power as well, but their actions speak louder. It is okay to feel happy, helpless, disgusted, ecstatic, sad, undecided, shocked, stubborn, or embarrassed. Maybe you feel bored, optimistic, shy, curious, angry, annoyed, hopeful, proud, or interested. It is quite alright to feel aggressive, puzzled, mischievous, withdrawn, regretful, frightened, guilty, thoughtful, or frustrated. How you, or the people around you, act out those emotions is important. There are helpful (and not so helpful) ways to express our emotions.

The *American Heritage Steadman's Medical Dictionary* online defines trauma as "a bodily injury or shock as from violence or an accident." Trauma is also defined as "a severely disturbing experience that leads to lasting psychological or emotional impairment." Trauma can become the lens that we see everything through. Overcoming our trauma helps us recognize that some terrible things happened, but we can be healed and made whole once again.

This book will help those who have experienced trauma to realize you are not alone, you can be healed, and you can experience freedom in every area of your life. The healing process is different for everyone. Some people might only take a short amount of time. Others may take longer, but the fact remains that God, Abba, wants to heal us. He wants us to walk in freedom.

As you read, you will notice I say Abba. During the course of these events, you will read about how my relationship with Abba, the Trinity (Father, Son, and Holy Spirit), grew. I came across Romans 8:15 that says, *"…we can cry out 'Abba, Father…'"* The footnote in *The Passion Translation* states:

> Abba is not a Greek word, but an Aramaic word transliterated into Greek letters. Abba is the Aramaic word for "father." It is also found in Mark 14:36 and Galatians 4:6. Abba is **also** a word for devotion, a term of endearment. This is why some have concluded that Abba could be translated as "Daddy" or "Papa." It is hard to imagine a closer relationship to have with God than to call him "Abba, our Beloved Father."

When I came across this, I was in desperate need of a Daddy. I began asking Abba about everything, and I still do. Therefore, when I say "Abba," I am referring to Father God, Papa God, Almighty God, Yahweh, Creator of Heaven and Earth, the Ancient of Days.

I was introduced to Christ at a young age. There were many things I did not understand and had a lot of fears. One of them was speaking in front of people; another was being put under water. Due to both of these fears, I was fourteen when I made a public confession for Christ during the first sermon of a relative and was baptized. I only remember being at the back of the sanctuary, finding myself walking forward, and sitting in a chair facing the crowd. Little did I know how significant this event was in my life.

Now that I am free from the trauma I experienced from childhood into young adulthood, I want to walk you through my journey towards freedom. What qualifies me? Let's find out in chapter one.

In high school, I started writing because I did not know how to talk about emotions. Writing also became one of the ways I talk to Abba. Through daily writing, Abba began telling me that my voice needs to be heard. He also said, "It is time. Your writing is going to be intentional. You must share your story so others can get free." *"Therefore if any man be in Christ, he is a new creature: old things are passed away; behold, all things are become new."*     2 Corinthians 5:17 (KJV)

To the reader of this book, your next mission, if you choose to accept it, is to become an overcomer. Dictionary.com defines overcome as "to get the better of in a struggle or conflict." I invite you to come along on this journey to freedom. It may not be a quick work, but it is definitely worth it. The Apostle Paul encourages us with these words:

*"We are pressed on every side by troubles, but we are not crushed and broken. We are perplexed, but we don't give up and quit. We are hunted down, but God never abandons us. We get knocked down, but we get up again and keep going."*
                                        2 Corinthians 4:8-9 (NLT)

Freedom awaits you, my friend. *"He who began a good work in you will complete it,"* according to Philippians 1:6 (NKJV). Come, my friend, let us make this journey together.

# 1

## DEAL WITH THE LIES

*"For you are the children of your father the devil, and you love to do the evil things he does. He was a murderer from the beginning. He has always hated the truth, because there is no truth in him. When he lies, it is consistent with his character; for he is a liar and the father of lies."*

John 8:44 (NLT)

### WHO CREATES THE LIES?

The above Bible verse says the devil creates lies, speaks them, and will keep speaking them. He wants us to feel sorry for ourselves. The devil does not want us to be around other people who will speak truth to us. Nor does he want us around people who will say, "That happened to me too." The devil kept me separated from my destiny because I believed his lies as I did not know the truth. I had no one to tell me the truth.

### WHERE DO LIES ORIGINATE?

Lies originate from the enemy, the devil. These lies are intended to keep us out of relationships or hinder our relationships with others. Dictionary.com defines a lie like this: "a false statement made with deliberate intent to deceive; an intentional untruth." We have a real enemy who wages war against us (1 Peter 5:8). The lies I once believed began when I was five years old: "no one will listen," "you are too young," "no one will believe you," and "it does not matter." The lies continued and were magnified when I was seventeen. These lies originated in the pit of hell. They are not the truth.

> *"So Jesus said to the Jews who had believed him, 'If you abide in my word, you are truly my disciples, and you will know the truth, and the truth will set you free.'"*
>
> John 8:31-32 (ESV)

We must learn to recognize the lies and replace them with the truth. Merriam-Webster.com defines truth as: "a judgment, proposition, or idea that is true or accepted as true." The Word of God, the Holy Bible, gives us truth. Truth is a fundamental characteristic of God. John 1:14 (ESV) states, *"Jesus, as the Word became flesh ...is full of grace and truth."* Jesus describes Himself in John 14:6 (ESV) *"...as the way, the truth, and the life."* The Holy Spirit reveals truth to replace lies when we are alone. The enemy—meaning the devil, Satan, (and those he uses)--wants us to think that we are alone so that he can continue to feed us lies. Believing them makes us have the wrong thoughts about ourselves and possibly even other people. I was believing many lies.

You see, when I was young, I was molested; and then, just three years after my public confession of Christ, my Daddy was murdered. Now that I am free, I want to walk you through my journey towards freedom from trauma by addressing the traumas of being molested and losing a parent to murder. The Cambridge Dictionary defines molest this way: "to touch someone sexually when it is not wanted." When I was about five, a teenager molested me. My family was visiting some friends we had known for a long time. The adults were in the kitchen and the children were in the living room watching TV. I had no idea how this event would impact the next thirty years of my life.

Suffocation is a scary feeling. There have been so many times in my life where I felt like I could not breathe. Under a blanket in a living room where I should have been safe, that's how I felt. I am only aware of it happening one time. He told me not to tell and I never did. In fact, I did not remember this happening until two months before going to the other side of the world. When it surfaced, I asked Abba some questions about it. He answered all of them, and I gave the whole situation to Him. I chose to forgive the perpetrator.

*The combination of trauma, lies, and fear were controlling my family, but we did not know it.*

I was upset about the lies I began believing because of this incident. For over thirty years, I told myself: "no one will listen," "you are too young," "no one will believe you," and "it does not matter." These lies were shouted over and over in my head. At this time, fear came in as well. I began to believe the lies while I operated through fear. Not long after this traumatic event, I began to have serious breathing issues. Fear also started to grip my parents as well. I had a lot of breathing issues due to asthma. It appeared that just about everything set it off: if I got too hot or too cold, if I ran, was around cigarette smoke, ate corn nuts, laughed too hard, etc. I spent a lot of time in the emergency room and on the pediatric floor of our local hospital. I would visit the ER so often that they kept my chart handy.

The combination of trauma, lies, and fear were controlling my family, but we did not know it. Instead of talking about emotions, I just stopped feeling. I was in a lot of pain physically and emotionally. I do not remember anyone in my immediate family talking about emotions. As if my young life could not get any worse, shortly after my seventeenth birthday, my Daddy was murdered while I was visiting relatives in Oklahoma. This completely changed my world. The lies that entered when I was five had just been doused with gasoline. Now add to that the high-profile, violent murder of my father and you have a very toxic person.

My trauma story led to the creation of this book. I realized that I was not experiencing all that Abba had for me. I began to search for what was missing. Through staying connected with the local Body of Believers, I began to learn more about the Holy Spirit. I found out that there was much more available to me than I had been previously taught.

All along, fear was controlling me, and these lies were still playing in my head: "no one will listen," "you are too young," "no one will believe you," and "it does not matter." They were not as loud as before, but still there. I heard them so often that I became accustomed to hearing them. Perhaps I thought they were my own thoughts.

I would learn new things about the Bible, Abba (God), Jesus, Holy Spirit, healing, and freedom. I would make progress, and then stop. It was like taking five steps forward and three steps back. I am not a quitter, so I kept trying. Being a good student, I know how to follow directions. Others were encouraging me with joy and laughter and I could envision those things, but it just had not happened naturally yet. I began asking Abba more questions, and told Him I wanted to be free. Free to express myself, to learn how to communicate, and to discover "the more" that I needed to know about Abba.

At seventeen, I started going to counseling. This is where the process of learning about emotions started. As a result of the internal and external pressures of the fear and lies, I began to hear voices implying that I end my life. I did not act on this but told a trusted adult. As a result, I spent a week on a psychiatric ward. The voices were saying, "It doesn't matter." Even though I knew this was a lie, I still did not recognize the other lies.

As I write this, I am seeing the connection to the lies and fear that started around age five. Three of the lies: "no one will listen," "no one will believe you," and "it does not matter" coupled with fear were in full operation during my grief process. I felt like no one had ever really listened to me before my Daddy's death, so why would they now? But once I spoke out about the voices implying to end my life, several people took notice.

I am so thankful that I was already in counseling. At the beginning, I did not talk. I would sit in silence or cry silent tears. Unless I learned about my emotions and how to communicate them, it became clear to me that I could die. I had experienced so much trauma that I was not sure if I was going to implode or explode. I believe those closest to me wondered the same thing. When these voices were basically telling me to kill myself, I had to sound the alarm. I was afraid to die. I disliked the feeling that came over me when I heard these voices.

The week in the psychiatric ward helped me to recognize that I had a support system. Abba had surrounded me with people in and out of my biological family that cared deeply about me. Some of them, like me, did not know how to communicate feelings and emotions very well, but their actions let me know how much they cared. I am forever grateful for the love and support I have been shown, and know that's one of the reasons I am still here.

A prayer I have is that one day they too will experience this freedom. Freedom to express all the emotions they have felt, and that it is okay to feel that way. Even the Bible says to *"...be angry and do not sin"* in Ephesians 4:26 (ESV). Our emotions are from Abba, our Creator. What we choose to do as a result of those emotions may or may not cause problems.

Open, honest communication with someone you trust is a way to deal with and avoid lies, and being transparent will help expose any lies that are there. Due to trauma at a young age, I can now see that I did not trust people, and this breakdown in relationships with others allowed seeds of doubt to be planted along with the lies.

---

*This breakdown in relationships with others allowed seeds of doubt to get planted along with the lies.*

---

From the beginning of time, the devil has used lies and doubt to cause breakdowns in relationships. Do you remember Adam and Eve? This happened to them too. The devil caused them to doubt what the Father said. This doubt led to disobedience, which then caused a break in their relationship that cost them everything.

Now is a good time to pause and ask the Holy Spirit: What fundamental lie or lies shaped me incorrectly that You want to reveal? Jot down what you hear. We will come back to this.

_____
_____
_____
_____
_____
_____

## WHY IS IT IMPORTANT TO DEAL WITH LIES?

*"You brood of vipers! How can you speak good, when you are evil? For out of the abundance of the heart the mouth speaks."*

Matthew 12:34 (ESV)

It is important to deal with lies and replace them with truths, because lies will mess up our relationships. Quite possibly, they can lead us down the wrong path and become interwoven into everything we do. Lies are meant to cause us doubt. They can also isolate us by making us think we are alone and no one else is experiencing what we are. No one is an island. If it happened to you, there are other people who experience or have experienced the same or remarkably similar things. Help is available. Hebrews 13:5b (ESV) assures us *"...for he has said, "I will never leave you nor forsake you.""*

## HOW DO YOU DEAL WITH THE LIES?

*"I beseech you therefore, brethren, by the mercies of God, that you present your bodies a living sacrifice, holy, acceptable to God, which is your reasonable service. And do not be conformed to this world, but be transformed by the renewing of your mind, that you may prove what is that good and acceptable and perfect will of God."*

Romans 12:1-2 (NKJV)

The lies must be replaced with the truth. The four lies I believed were: "no one will listen," "I am too young," "no one will believe me," and "it does not matter." The truth is: people will listen because I have a voice, I was created for such a time as this, many will believe me, and everything concerning me matters to Abba. Ask Abba to show these truths to you in His Word. Write them out, memorize them, post them around your house, in your car, and at work. Say them daily OUT LOUD until the false statements are replaced with judgments, propositions, or ideas that are true or accepted as true.

> *"For my thoughts are not your thoughts, neither are your ways my ways, declares the Lord. For as the heavens are higher than the earth, so are my ways higher than your ways and my thoughts than your thoughts."*
>
> Isaiah 55:8-9 (ESV)

What lies did the Holy Spirit reveal to you earlier? Now let us ask Him: What is the truth? Be sure to jot down what you hear.

_____
_____
_____
_____
_____
_____
_____
_____
_____

Journal Entry:

While most of my senior year of high school was a blur, I will never forget Labor Day weekend, given that it was the last time I saw my Daddy. Some members of my family and I left early Saturday morning for Oklahoma City. He was doing something at the sink, so his back was to me when I left the kitchen. If I had known that was the last time I would see him,

I would have given him a big hug, and told him how much he meant to me. But I did not, so I just left.

I do not remember much of the trip. It was one we had taken before. I have many relatives in Oklahoma City, and we always have a good time when we get together. The weather was always warmer in Oklahoma than in Kansas. The main thing I remember is not sleeping well Sunday night, and it was cold Monday morning, the temperature having made a 40-degree drop. You needed a coat and frost was on everything outside, and I felt like I was moving in slow motion. I knew something was wrong, just not what.

I was sitting up front with the driver. Perhaps I helped drive, I don't remember. We arrived back at the Topeka toll booth just fine. As we were headed to the house, we noticed my brother-in-law driving in the opposite direction with our Pastor. [Later, we learned that they had planned to meet us at the toll booth before we arrived at a house full of people.] We proceeded on to the house. When we turned off the main road two blocks away, we could see lots of cars at our house. We drove on. When we turned the corner, we found one spot open and my sister-in-law sitting on the porch. We parked and people came to the vehicle. They told us that Daddy was shot and killed last night.

I am not sure how I ended up in my bedroom. I felt like I was in a bad dream and could not wake up. It seemed as if my heart had been ripped out, I had been turned upside down and shaken, and then turned right side back up. How was I to function now?

Eventually, I went back to school because I needed something else to do, but my mind was not there. I was going through the motions. One of the social workers at the school was extremely helpful. She gave me a Steno notebook and told me to write. I did little talking during my grief. While I had a lot of emotions raging through me, I did not know how to talk about them, but knew I had to learn how to express them or I was going to die...literally. The pain was excruciating.

As I reviewed my journals to complete this book, I see Scripture, music, family, and friends helped me finish that last year of high school. Somewhere during all of this, violence in the city had increased. Many people, especially youths, were dying due to gun violence. A group of students came together to do something about it. Our mess became our message. With the help of some school officials and our community, we wrote, directed, and produced "Dreams Die Young." I learned many lessons by collaborating with others, and began to find my voice in writing. A few lessons learned: It is good to listen to what others have been through, it is good to cry, and writing is healing. By the grace of Abba, I graduated that May.

Journal Entry:

> My two years in Washington, DC were a true learning experience. Overall, I had a great time and would not trade it for anything, even though I would make some better choices if I had to do it over. I was in pain and trying to fill the hole in my heart. I had many flings instead of healthy relationships. There were even times when I was willing to sell my body to buy essentials. I thought I was up against the wall and this was my only choice.
> 
> Everyone said just the right things that my ears and heart needed to hear at that time, but there was no attraction whatsoever in any of them. What was I thinking? Well, I was not thinking, and that was the problem. I did not want to dwell on any of the issues any longer. I wanted to be freed from all of them. Am I willing to ask Abba and trust Him on this one?

Do you trust Him? Is He big enough to handle all of your issues? Sometimes we believe lies based on sins that were committed against us. As a result, we often make a vow. These sins and vows are not based on the truth. Certain things done to us affect our heart. Earlier, we asked the Holy Spirt about lies we believe. Let us take a moment now to ask Abba to give us a clean heart. Ask Him to expose and remove everything in our heart that is not from Him. Do not get in a hurry. Allow Abba to scrub your heart and mind of the lies you have believed for so long. *"Create in me a clean heart, O God; and renew a right spirit within me"* Psalm 51:10 (KJV). This step is vital before we begin replacing the lies. This is foundational to the rest of this book.

If you want to be free, you cannot skip this step. Lies told and any vows made must be exposed for healing to come. Allow Abba to show you the root. Once it has been identified, we know how to combat it. All lies must be replaced with the truth. The truth is what Abba says. We must make declarations using the Bible. I encourage you to write them out, say them out loud, post them around your house, car, and work area, and memorize them. Here are a few Scriptures to get you started. **These are only suggestions.** Ask the Holy Spirit to help you write declarations specific to your situation.

## DECLARATIONS

2 Timothy 1:7 (NKJV) *For God has not given us a spirit of fear, but of power and of love and of a sound mind.*

I declare God has not given me a spirit of fear, but of power, love, and a sound mind.

Jeremiah 31:3 (ESV) *the Lord appeared to him from far away. I have loved you with an everlasting love; therefore I have continued my faithfulness to you.*

I declare the Lord loves me, (insert your name), with an everlasting love. He is faithful to me.

Revelation 12:11 (KJV) *And they overcame him by the blood of the Lamb, and by the word of their testimony; and they loved not their lives unto the death.*

I declare I, (insert your name), will overcome by the blood of the Lamb and the word of my testimony.

Philippians 1:6 (NIV) *being confident of this, that he who began a good work in you will carry it on to completion until the day of Christ Jesus.*

I decree and declare He who began a good work in (insert your name) will carry it on to completion until the day of Christ Jesus.

Colossians 3:1-3 (NKJV) *If then you were raised with Christ, seek those things which are above, where Christ is, sitting at the right hand of God. Set your mind on things above, not on things on the earth. For you died, and your life is hidden with Christ in God.*

I declare just as I was raised with Christ, I will set my mind on things above, not on things on this earth. For (insert your name)'s life is hidden with Christ in God.

Philippians 4:8 (ESV) *Finally, brothers, whatever is true, whatever is honorable, whatever is just, whatever is pure, whatever is lovely, whatever is commendable, if there is any excellence, if there is anything worthy of praise, think about these things.*

I declare I will think on praise worthy things that are true, honorable, just, pure, lovely, commendable and excellent.

Psalm 141:3 (ESV) *Set a guard, O Lord, over my mouth; keep watch over the door of my lips!*

I decree and declare the Lord sets a guard over my mouth. I declare the Lord is helping (insert your name) only speak beautiful words over others.

Here is **an example** of putting it all together:

> I declare God has not given me a spirit of fear, but of power, love, and a sound mind. The Lord loves me, (insert your name), with an everlasting love. He is faithful to me. I declare I, (insert your name), will overcome by the blood of the Lamb and the word of my testimony. I decree and declare He who began a good work in me, (insert your name), will carry it on to completion until the day of Christ Jesus. Just as I was raised with Christ, I will set my mind on things above, not on things on this earth. For (insert your name)'s life is hidden with Christ in God. I declare I will think on things that are worthy of praise, true, honorable, just, pure, lovely, commendable and excellent. I decree and declare the Lord sets a guard over my mouth. Thank you Lord for helping me, (insert your name), only speak beautiful words over others. Amen.

Check the Resource section for more examples of declarations.

# 2

## GET OUT OF THE BOX

Expanding the view of ourselves is important according to how our Creator, Almighty God sees us. Each person is different or distinct in nature, and was created with certain character traits, gifts, and graces that are unique. Even when people have the same traits, each one will display them in a unique way. We each display a different aspect of our Creator, Almighty God (Abba). Our experiences also make us different, which is a good thing, as one distinction is not better than the other. No one else will bring your uniqueness. Thank you for not being like everyone else in character or quality.

*Go ahead and rock your lane to encourage others to discover theirs.*

The Bible says, *"we are each fearfully and wonderfully made"* in Psalms 139 (ESV). First Corinthians 12 (NIV) tells us *"we are all part of the same body."* The hand cannot do the job of the foot. The ear cannot do the job of the hip. Each part has a unique, different job.

In the same way, each person is different and has a unique job, role, or destiny in life. You are the unique expression of Abba in the Earth. Genesis 1 (NKJV) says, *"let us make man in Our image."*

No one else can do what YOU were put here to do. It is time for the world to see what has been put on the inside of YOU. We need to see who YOU really are. YOU are unique. Stay in your lane, DO what Abba, Almighty Creator God, has put in YOU to do. Own it. Own who He has created YOU to be. Go ahead and rock your lane to encourage others to discover theirs. The world needs ALL of the expressions of Abba, Creator God, that are inside of you. He is very multi-faceted. Those expressions came out of His heart to be put on display in the Earth. It is okay to be different because no one person has all of His traits. Paul tells us in Philippians 1:6 (NKJV), *"Being confident of this very thing, that He who has begun a good work in you will complete it until the day of Jesus Christ."*

Now that our view has been expanded, we can determine if we have put ourselves in a box or allowed others to put us in a box.

## HOW WAS THE BOX CREATED?

My box was created when people put limitations on me. Some of these limitations were: my age, my size, my race, and because I did not talk a lot. When I saw myself the way others saw me, I agreed with the box. One day, I heard Abba say to me, "remove the limits." If I am going to remove the limits from what He can do, I need to also remove the limits that I have put on myself, and what other people have put on me. The limits are coming off and we are breaking out of the box! There is so much more to be done, to be explored, and to reach for than what is in the box. I want to have the freedom to be all that He has created me to be. Get out of the box! Get out of those old mindsets! Do not let anyone tell you that you cannot do something. *"Do not despise prophecies, but test everything; hold fast what is good"* 1 Thessalonians 5:20-21(ESV).

---

*The world needs ALL of the expressions of Abba, Creator God, that are inside of you.*

---

Abba likes adventure. I have been on countless adventures with Him by getting out of the box. If I would have stayed in the box, I would have never been to so many different places. Adventures with Abba has taken me to nine other countries. I have also experienced numerous adventures with Abba within the United States. My most recent one was to northwest Arkansas. With Abba, I have the most amazing time! I do not know the plans, but He does. I choose to trust Him because He told me to remove the limits. I have met so many different people because I decided to get out of the box. Life is full of adventures! If you stay in the box, you might miss out on how much there is to offer in this wide world that we live in.

## HOW DOES ONE GET OUT OF THE BOX?

In order to get out of the box, I started searching for more and immersed myself in the Bible. If I saw it in the Word, I believed I could have it too. I began to ask for more. I asked for wisdom and fire. Fire to burn up all that was not like Abba. Wisdom to know what to do with what was left. I began to ask for people to teach me more about the gifts available to us in 1 Corinthians 12.

Journal Entry:

Today was a mask day but it broke twice. I can't keep this up. So where shall I begin? I had felt like cursing the day that I was born. I can't blame God. I see Him there but I can't go to Him because He wants something that I am afraid to give Him. I cannot risk the exposure of such secrets to just anyone. I have asked Him, rather pleaded with Him, to come in the flesh. I would rather not end up in a hospital again. Being in the hospital will not help deliver me from my lack of trust or loose me from the strongholds of past sin or help heal my heart. I know what I need to do, but I cannot seem to do it.

As I look back to 1993, I see that I shut down emotionally and became busy. Anything to preoccupy my mind and not think about my emotions. It is easier to not deal with anything. But is that healthy? I remember sitting in the social worker's office as she told me about a giant bee in a jar. He kept bumping around, hitting itself against the sides and top, becoming more upset. There is more room on the outside than on the inside.

This began a long process of learning how to deal with life. It was a painstakingly slow ordeal. Many months, events, and the making of "Dreams Die Young" showed much improvement. Graduation and moving to DC followed.

## **WHY SHOULD SOMEONE GET OUT OF THE BOX?**

Have you ever seen a bumblebee in a jar? In this small, cramped space, the bumblebee is not able to fly to plants and flowers, collecting pollen and nectar from all the plants and flowers it visits. It is not able to do what it was created to do, because the jar limits the bumblebee's purpose. The box is the same. Outside of the box is freedom to soar, dream big dreams, and enlarge your territory. The sky is the limit for what you can do. You have a destiny, and it is far greater than you can imagine. Get out of the box!

> *He is very multi-faceted. Those expressions came out of His heart to be put on display in the Earth.*

At some point in my life, I felt like there was more available to me. Something was blocking me from being able to receive all that Abba had for me. I had heard that there are books about me in Heaven and a room that has presents for me. Why couldn't I get those presents down here? What was written in those books about me? Why didn't I get the results that others did when I did all that leaders told me to do? Having these questions made me think that something was in the way. I decided I would let Abba know I wanted to be free. I wanted to be free from whatever was blocking me from receiving ALL that He had for me.

## WHAT ARE THE IMPLICATIONS OF STAYING IN THE BOX?

Some implications of staying in the box include: being relegated to doing the same old thing; missing out on meeting really interesting people and going to extraordinary and exciting places; and not experiencing all that Abba has in store for you. If you stay in the box, you will not get to take a risk, and you let other people tell you what you can and cannot do. Personally, because I like adventure, I am breaking out of the box. To stay in the box would be robbing oneself of fantastic adventures.

Now is a good time to pause and ask the Holy Spirit: Have others put me in a box? Have I put myself in a box? Have I put the Creator of the Universe in a box? How do I remove the limits? Jot down what you hear.

_____

_____

_____

_____

_____

_____

_____

_____

# 3

# DETERMINE THAT OBEDIENCE IS BETTER THAN COMFORT

## WHAT DOES IT MEAN TO BE OBEDIENT?

You can set your face like flint towards the Lord and His will for you. To be obedient means that you obey what is asked of you. I am talking about being obedient to what Abba has said to do. He has told me, "you have a voice," "you have a story to tell," and "now is the time." Although there are parts of my story that I am not comfortable talking about, I would much rather do what He has asked me, than not to. There's no point in putting up a fight because I have been down that road before and He's going to win! I may be uncomfortable, but I desire to be free, and in order for me to be free, I have to share my story. He wants it in book form, and I am going to be obedient.

> *"You saw me before I was born. Every day of my life was recorded in your book. Every moment was laid out before a single day had passed."*

In my early twenties, I had a guy friend. We had good conversations and laughed a lot. We had mutual friends and saw each other often. Abba told me we were not to have a romantic relationship. I did not listen. I was very hurt by some of his choices. In the end, I lost my friend. If I would have chosen to obey Abba, I could have avoided some needless heartache. Thank You, Lord, for rescuing me out of that relationship. It felt so right but it was so very wrong. I learned a lot about myself by going through all that happened in that relationship. Eight years after it ended, I learned and saw how desperate I was for love and attention, but the problem was I went looking in the wrong places. I did not realize I was looking for love or attention. Around the year 2000, I learned it was better to be obedient than it was to make sacrifices. I could have saved myself a lot of heartache and heartbreak by being obedient. Our flesh should not rule us. Abba's ways are much better, much higher, and so much greater for us.

## WHERE DOES ONE LEARN OBEDIENCE?

I believe you learn obedience by living in community. Your community might be your family, your neighbors, people in your dorm, your church, your small group, or a community group that you are a part of. For every action, there's a reaction. Sometimes those reactions have positive consequences and sometimes those reactions have negative consequences. As we choose to obey (or not), we learn the effects of obedience. Ultimately, most of us learn obedience at a young age in our families taught by our parents, grandparents, and caregivers.

Philippians 4:13 (GNT) reads, *"I have the strength to face all conditions by the power that Christ gives me."* I believe this is a lesson Abba wants us to learn on our faith journey. I had to go to Vasquez, Guatemala and tackle the mountain He created in the scenery so

I would have the confidence to take on the "mountains" in my own life. The places the team needed to go—school, radio station, and church—were all up the mountain. If you went up, you had to come back down the mountain. We were coming back from doing Children's Church when it started raining. The rain was making the road slippery and it was getting dark. To make matters worse, one of my contacts came out, which made it difficult to see well. I had to trust our guide and lean into the Lord.

The things that seemed like mountains in my life were a research project and an internship in St. Louis, Missouri. Just like I had to choose to trust our guide and lean into the Lord in Guatemala, I had to do the same here. I had to choose to trust Him for wisdom and clarity on what were the next steps. Thank You, Lord, for Your word and the lessons You have taught me.

## WHEN IS OBEDIENCE BETTER THAN COMFORT?

*"You saw me before I was born. Every day of my life was recorded in your book. Every moment was laid out before a single day had passed."*

Psalm 139:16 (NLT)

*"The steps of a [good and righteous] man are directed and established by the Lord."*

Psalm 37:23a (Amplified Bible)

We can only see the present and the past. Abba sits outside of time. He knows the beginning from the end. When Abba created us, He gave us free will. We have the power to choose what we will do. We can choose to partner with Abba and cooperate with His plans or not.

Obedience is better than comfort when our comfort is not going to help us achieve a goal that Abba has laid on our hearts. For example, one of my goals is to be free. In order for me to experience a new level of freedom, there are things that I need to do that I have not done before which are probably not going to feel good. If I really want to have freedom in areas I have not had before, I need to make a conscious decision to be obedient to whatever the authority figure is asking me to do. In my case, Abba said to share my story and write a book that helps people change.

Being comfortable will not help you achieve your purpose. Esther had a choice to make. The Bible says in Esther 4:11-14 (NLT),

*"The whole world knows that anyone who appears before the king in his inner court without being invited is doomed to die unless the king holds out his gold scepter. And the king has not called for me to come to him in more than a month." So Hathach gave Esther's message to Mordecai. Mordecai sent back this reply to Esther: "Don't think for a moment that you will escape there in the palace when all other Jews are killed. If you keep quiet at a time like this, deliverance for the Jews will arise from some other place, but you and your relatives will die. What's more, who can say but you have been elevated to the palace for just such a time as this?"*

Esther was extremely comfortable in the palace and had to make a decision. Here is her reply:

*"Go, and gather together all the Jews of Susa and fast for me. Do not eat or drink for three days, night or day. My maids and I will do the same. And then, **though it is against the law, I will go in to see the king. If I must die, I am willing to die**"* Esther 4:16 (NLT emphasis added).

You will have to choose. Will you choose to be comfortable or will you choose to be obedient? First Samuel 15:23a (KJV) tells us that, *"rebellion is as the sin of witchcraft."* Merriam-Webster.com defines rebellion as: "opposition to one in authority or dominance." Abba is inviting you to partner with Him to receive something you have not had yet. You must make a choice. I want to encourage you to be obedient to what He is inviting you to do.

Now is a good time to pause and ask the Holy Spirit: What do I need to do to be obedient to what the Father has told me to do? Jot down what you hear.

_____
_____
_____
_____
_____
_____
_____
_____
_____

I was briefly on assignment as a Children's Pastor in my early thirties. I combined fasting with prayer in order to make sure I heard about this position correctly. This was not something I wanted; however, my desire to be obedient was much greater than my desire to be comfortable. While in this position, I was teaching part time at an elementary school. There were many short nights because these jobs both required preparation time. While there was much opposition, Abba confirmed that this was where I was meant to be. I was out of my comfort zone, but I was obediently leaning into Him to show me the way. This assignment lasted a little over a year.

What I discovered was that my identity was wrapped up in teaching. That is not who I am—that is something I do. Abba took the summer to unravel this thinking and take me deeper in Him and His Word. At the end of that year, after many tears, I gave up all my dreams as an act of obedience just as Abba asked me to.

# 4

# RECOGNIZE WHO ABBA CREATED YOU TO BE

## HOW DOES A PERSON LEARN WHO THEY WERE CREATED TO BE?

It is never "too early" to start cultivating a relationship with Abba. Having faith like a child will make the process smoother. Colossians 2:6-7 (ESV) reminds us: *"Therefore, as you received Christ Jesus the Lord, so walk in him, rooted and built up in him and established in the faith, just as you were taught, abounding in thanksgiving."* Ask Abba who He created you to be. What purpose did He have in mind when He created you? The prophet Isaiah tells us in chapter 49 (ESV): *"Listen to me, O coastlands, and give attention, you peoples from afar. The Lord called me from the womb, from the body of my mother he named my name."* A question that I asked for many years was what is my role in the Kingdom? There are many assessments of spiritual gifts that you can take, and you can also think about your passion and natural abilities.

Words have power. The Bible tells us in Proverbs 18:21 (ESV), *"Death and life are in the power of the tongue and those who love it will eat its fruit."* I encourage you to look up the meaning of your name. A name describes the authority or strength of something. You get to choose what your name means. A name can be changed in an instant. You get to agree with what the world says, or with what Abba says. He has given us the authority to choose. Once Abba tells us what we were created for, we have the opportunity to become all we were meant to be from the beginning of time. Once we know the meaning of our name, the essence of who we are can strengthen the meaning.

My oldest sister named me. She heard it and liked it. When she asked our parents if she could name me, they said yes. Many people have asked me the meaning, but I did not know. When I was in my mid-thirties, I discovered the meaning of my name. Once I read it, I thought, "How interesting!" Then I looked up the definitions to the words. I said, "This is the story of my life." Here is the meaning of Marteka:

Swahili for patience, long suffering, perseverance and to believe in.

**patience**= an ability or willingness to suppress restlessness or annoyance when confronted with delay; quiet, steady perseverance; diligence

**long suffering**= love on trial that enables you to forbear and forgive patiently enduring wrongs or difficulties

**perseverance**= steady persistence in a course of action, purpose, state etc., in spite of difficulties, obstacles or discouragement

**believe**= to have confidence in the truth, the existence, or the reliability of something, although without absolute proof that one is right in doing so

Perhaps when you discover or rediscover the meaning of your name, you will receive some clarity. The Holy Spirit is the revealer of truth. Feel free to also ask Him who you were created to be.

## WHAT HAPPENS IF A PERSON NEVER DISCOVERS THEIR CREATED PLACE?

If a person never discovers their created place, they will feel like something is missing. The first thirty-one and a half years of my life had been marked by fear of rejection, many insecurities, lack of trust, lack of affirmation or validation, anxiety, sorrow, brokenness, false comforts, no sense of identity, and no voice of love and blessing. The next eighteen months were marked by Abba preparing to heal me of all of these. It's simple, but it's not easy. I had to have a paradigm shift. Now I look at life through a different set of lenses. Part of the preparation included people coming into my life for "wound care" to help me heal. I am very thankful for all the people Abba sent into my life. Because of the lies I was believing, I did not know who I was or where I belonged.

## WHY IS IT IMPORTANT TO KNOW AND RECOGNIZE WHO ABBA CREATED YOU TO BE?

*"Consider it pure joy, my brothers and sisters, whenever you face trials of many kinds, because you know that the testing of your faith produces perseverance. Let perseverance finish its work so that*

*you may be mature and complete, not lacking anything. If any of you lacks wisdom, you should ask God, who gives generously to all without finding fault, and it will be given to you. But when you ask, you must believe and not doubt, because the one who doubts is like a wave of the sea, blown and tossed by the wind. That person should not expect to receive anything from the Lord."*

James 1:2-7 (NIV)

Once you know who you were created to be, you can start learning more about it. Things will begin to "just click" and line up. While at Wichita State University, I began to pray, "the world is my classroom." I did not realize that I prayed this out loud until someone was praying for me and they said it. I asked them why. They responded, "You always say that." As I think back over my life and all the things I have done, Abba, You have prepared me for such a time as this.

*"Then he showed me Joshua the high priest standing before the angel of the Lord, and Satan standing at his right side to accuse him. The Lord said to Satan, "The Lord rebuke you, Satan! The Lord, who has chosen Jerusalem, rebuke you! Is not this man a burning stick snatched from the fire?" Now Joshua was dressed in filthy clothes as he stood before the angel. The angel said to those who were standing before him, "Take off his filthy clothes." Then he said to Joshua, "See, I have taken away your sin, and I will put fine garments on you." Then I said, "Put a clean turban on his head." So, they put a clean turban on his head and clothed him, while the angel of the Lord stood by. The angel of the Lord gave this charge to Joshua: "This is what the Lord Almighty says: 'If you will walk in obedience to me and keep my requirements, then you will govern my house and have charge of my courts, and I will give you a place among these standing here."*

Zechariah 3:1-7 (NIV)

Satan, the accuser of the brethren, constantly throws our pasts in our faces. The angel of the Lord took our sin (filthy clothes) and our old mindset (dirty turbans). In exchange, He gave us fine garments and a clean turban. The Lord Jesus Christ of Nazareth Who came in the flesh took our place. His holy blood covers our sin. We have the mind of Christ. Through daily communication, we learn to hear the voice of the Lord clearly, learn to recognize the lies, learn obedience, and learn about our destiny—who we were created to be.

Now is a good time to pause and reflect. Do you see yourself in fine garments and a clean turban? Ask the Holy Spirit: Who was I created to be? Jot down what you hear.

_____
_____
_____
_____
_____
_____
_____
_____
_____

# 5

## LEARN TO ACCEPT FREEDOM

*"Now a slave has no permanent place in the family, but a son belongs to it forever. So if the Son sets you free, you will be free indeed."*

John 8:35-36 (NIV)

## WHAT DOES IT MEAN TO BE FREE?

Freedom is being like a child again. You have no worries and are free to express yourself in any way: dancing, singing, clapping, crying, laughing, and jumping. Being free is knowing who you are and being okay with it. Being free is believing in yourself. *"Out of my distress I called on the Lord; the Lord answered me and set me free."*

Psalm 118:5 (ESV)

## WHO DEFINES FREEDOM?

*"Now the Lord is the Spirit, and where the Spirit of the Lord is, there is freedom."*

2 Corinthians 3:17 (NIV)

The Oxford Dictionary defines freedom as a noun: "the power or right to act, speak, or think as one wants without hindrance or restraint." It goes on to say that freedom is also "the state of not being subject to or affected by (a particular undesirable thing)." How will you define your freedom? The lies have been exposed and replaced with the truth. The box you were in has been smashed because you decided that obedience is better than comfort. As a result of your obedience, you now have a better understanding of who you were created to be. You get to define your freedom. Yes, you know what freedom looks like to you. If not, ask the Holy Spirit.

---

*Freedom exposes the lies, replaces them with truth, realizes it is okay to be different, and helps you get out of the box.*

---

*"Who shall separate us from the love of Christ? Shall tribulation, or distress, or persecution, or famine, or nakedness, or danger, or sword? As it is written, "For your sake we are being killed all the day long; we are regarded as sheep to be slaughtered." No, in all these things we are more than conquerors through him who loved us. For I am sure that neither death nor life, nor angels nor rulers, nor things present nor things to come, nor powers, nor height nor depth, nor anything else in all creation, will be able to separate us from the love of God in Christ Jesus our Lord."*

Romans 8:35-39 (ESV)

## **FREEDOM**

What is freedom? What is independence?

When I think of freedom, I think of an open field, an open sky, children running, and babies laughing.

There are no chains, no snares, no ropes, no keys, no cages, no darkness, and no pain.

Freedom is enjoying the breeze, smelling the flowers, noticing colors and smells.

Freedom is dancing like no one is watching, crying because you are happy and going for a nice stroll.

Freedom is having no regrets.

Freedom is remembering good and bad things and knowing that it's okay.

Freedom is not having memories haunt you.

Freedom is seeing the good in people and circumstances.

Freedom is speaking out so your voice is heard.

Freedom is acknowledging your pain.

Freedom is forgiving those who have caused you pain.

Freedom is believing in yourself.

Freedom is believing there is One who created you.

Freedom is realizing you are distinctly and necessarily different.

Freedom is knowing who you are.

Independence is a gift.

But we were created to rely on One.

We were created to bring Him glory.

Oh yes, He wants us to be free.

Free of chains.

Free of hurts and trauma.

Free from destructive behaviors.

Free from thoughts that are wrong and not helpful for encouraging others.

He wants us free from pain.

Maybe that pain is in our physical body.

Maybe that pain is in our mind.

Maybe that pain is in our emotions.

Wherever the pain is, He wants us to give it to Him.

He came so we can experience freedom.

True freedom.

He will not pressure us. He will wait until we are ready.

You see, He gave us the freedom to choose.

We get to choose to hold onto that pain.

Sometimes we don't even know the pain is there.

But when it does come up, we have been given the power of choice.

What would it be like to be free of emotional pain?

What would it be like to be free of physical and mental pain?

The choice is up to you.

Will you accept the offer to live a life that you haven't before?

Maybe you once had freedom but now you're locked up with pain.

Freedom is knocking.

Freedom is available.

He offers freedom.

Freedom is a choice.

Will you choose freedom?

Will you give up your right to be right?

Will you give up wanting to get revenge?

Will you forgive those who hurt you?

What they did was wrong, but release them to the One Who is offering freedom.

Freedom is what I'm after.

Freedom in my mind.

Freedom in my body.

Freedom in my finances.

Freedom in my house.

Freedom in my relationships.

Freedom in my emotions.

Freedom in my family.

FREEDOM!!!

20/20 is perfect vision. I want to see clearly.

When I'm in pain, I can't see clearly.

There's something in the way.

Something is blocking my vision.

Pain can block vision.

Freedom is calling.

Can you hear it?

Can you see it?

No. Well, what pain is blocking you from seeing it?

He can remove what's blocking your vision.

The choice is up to you.

Freedom is available for 20/20 vision.

Freedom is available to hear sounds you've never heard before.

Freedom is available to do things you've never done before.

Freedom in your heart, your house, your finances, your relationships, your family, and your emotions is possible.

There is One Who paid it all.

All to Him I owe.

Freedom is calling.

Now is the time.

I want to be free.

Free like a bird.

Free to love in a new way.

Free to live in a new way.

Free to be who I was created to be.

Free to be happy.

Free to be carefree.

Free to enjoy life and those around me.

Oh let freedom ring!

FREEEEDOOOOOMMMMM!!

## HOW DOES A PERSON LEARN TO ACCEPT FREEDOM?

Each day, you will have multiple opportunities to choose freedom. Step one is allowing Abba to heal you. You must choose to allow Him to examine the deep recesses of your heart. He needs total access to begin to deal with the hurt that is there. More lies might be exposed, but now you know what to do with them.

You learn to accept freedom by trying new things. Explore your new found freedom and then evaluate how you feel. The choice is yours, but you have to make that choice. Once you are free, you can begin learning to enjoy freedom.

Freedom exposes the lies, replaces them with truth, realizes it is okay to be different, and helps you get out of the box. Your freedom may not look like the next person's freedom. In my early thirties, I experienced a cleansing year. Freedom came to my heart and life from many things, people, and relationships. It was not an easy road. Several people who I'd had relationships with for five to fifteen years were removed from my life. Letting them go was tough, but I had to be obedient. We were no longer going in the same direction. My heart was so exposed, and I felt lonely at times. This is when I began to understand that people are often only in your life for a season. Abba said, "Hold on just a little bit longer. I will come swiftly. I have heard your cry. I see every movement."

## WHY ACCEPT FREEDOM?

I believe you should accept freedom to discover who you really are. When we are bound up with issues, the issues consume us. They do not allow us to be who we were meant to be, who we were created to be.

When we accept help to get free of these issues that are consuming us and have us bound, we begin to discover who we really are. Maybe you have never met the real you? Maybe you need to rediscover what you like and do not like? Accepting freedom will help you to fulfill your destiny. You will be free to be who you were created to be.

Ask the Holy Spirit: What do I need to do in order to accept the freedom that the Lord Jesus Christ gave me? Jot down what you hear.

_____
_____
_____
_____
_____
_____
_____
_____
_____

# CONCLUSION

You are well on your way to freedom. Bad things happen in life, but you get to choose if you are going to let your emotions be in control or not. When we react, our emotions are in control of us. When we respond, we are in control of our emotions. There are times when we need help from others. No one is an island. We were created to live in community. Please reach out to those around you. You may even have to get some help from trained professionals. My friend, it is okay. We need you whole and healthy to fulfill your destiny.

---

*Bad things happen in life. You get to choose if you are going to let your emotions be in control or not.*

---

Let us review what we have done. With the help of the Holy Spirit, you have identified foundational lies that you were believing. Those have been replaced with truth. You have accepted your unique differences. You made the decision to remove the limits and get out of the box. As an act of obedience, you smashed the box you put yourself in and the one others put you in. You decided it was better to be obedient rather than be comfortable. All of this helped you get a clearer picture of who Abba created you to be. Then you had to choose to persevere.

Freedom awaits. Well done, my friend. You have now partnered with Abba to give you beauty for ashes.

> *"To console those who mourn in Zion, To give them beauty for ashes, The oil of joy for mourning, The garment of praise for the spirit of heaviness; That they may be called trees of righteousness, The planting of the Lord, that He may be glorified."*
>
> Isaiah 61:3 (NKJV)

Once you have put it all together, your destiny awaits. You now have a solid foundation. The cracks have been filled. You can finally breathe without any obstructions. Your vision has become crystal clear. You look and sound refreshed. The real you has emerged. The person that Abba created has finally arrived. The opinions of others no longer control you. You made the decision to put a greater value on what Abba says and thinks about you than what anyone else says or thinks. Congratulations! You really are a new creation!

---

**When we react, our emotions are in control of us. When we respond, we are in control of our emotions.**

---

The Apostle Paul tells us in 2 Corinthians 3:17-18 (ESV),

> *"Now the Lord is the Spirit, and where the Spirit of the Lord is, there is freedom. And we all, with unveiled face, beholding the glory of the Lord, are being transformed into the same image from one degree of glory to another. For this comes from the Lord who is the Spirit."*

Then later in 5:17 (NKJV) he says, *"Therefore, if anyone is in Christ, he is a new creation; old things have passed away; behold, all things have become new."*

When you are walking in your destiny, your circle of influence gets to benefit. Each day we get multiple opportunities to choose how to deal with the things that are coming our way. We get the choice to respond or react.

The trajectory of your situation has now changed. You and your family have some sharp tools to help you make better choices. Dictionary.com defines overcomer as "one who gets the better of in a struggle or conflict." Congratulations, mighty warrior. You are an overcomer!

> *"Brothers and sisters, I do not consider myself yet to have taken hold of it. But one thing I do:* **Forgetting what is behind** *and straining toward what is ahead,* **I press on toward the goal** *to win the prize for which God has called me heavenward in Christ Jesus."*
>
> Philippians 3:13-14 (NIV emphasis added)

# RESOURCES

Declarations open the ears of your spirit man to hear what Abba is saying about the situation versus what you want for the situation. Praying in the Spirit helps you hear clearly. Then say what you are hearing in faith, believing that His Word is powerful and effective.

Here is **an example** of a declaration made using Scripture from Joshua 1:5-9, Isaiah 40:27-31, and 41:8-13:

According to the Bible, I declare that My God, will always be with me; You will NEVER abandon me. You tell Your servant (insert your name) to be determined, be confident; and make sure that (s/he) obeys Father God. I declare I have no need to be afraid or discouraged, for the Lord my God is with me wherever I go.

The Lord is the everlasting God. He strengthens me, (insert your name), when I am weak and tired. I declare that when I trust in the Lord for help, You will renew my strength. I will rise on wings like eagles; I declare I will run, walk, and not grow weary or weak.

The Lord has brought me from the ends of the earth and said to me, "(insert your name), you are My servant, I chose you. I am the Lord your God; I strengthen you (insert your name) and tell you not to be afraid because I will help you."

Below is a short list of Scripture to help you get started on some declarations.

1 John 4:4 (NIV) *You, dear children, are from God and have overcome them, because the one who is in you is greater than the one who is in the world.*

Revelation 21:7 (NKJV) *He who overcomes shall inherit all things, and I will be his God and he shall be My son.*

1 John 4:18 (NKJV) *There is no fear in love; but perfect love casts out fear, because fear involves torment. But he who fears has not been made perfect in love.*

John 8:31-32 (NKJV) *Then Jesus said to those Jews who believed Him, "If you abide in My word, you are My disciples indeed. And you shall know the truth, and the truth shall make you free."*

John 15:5 (NKJV) *"I am the vine, you are the branches. He who abides in Me, and I in him, bears much fruit; for without Me you can do nothing.*

Romans 4:17 (KJV) *(As it is written, I have made thee a father of many nations,) before him whom he believed, even God, who quickeneth the dead, and calleth those things which be not as though they were.*

Ephesians 2:6 (NKJV) *and raised us up together, and made us sit together in the heavenly places in Christ Jesus.*

Romans 8:1-2 (NIV) *Therefore, there is now no condemnation for those who are in Christ Jesus, because through Christ Jesus the law of the Spirit who gives life has set you free from the law of sin and death.*

1 Thessalonians 1:4 (ESV) *For we know, brothers loved by God, that he has chosen you.*

Galatians 5:22-23 (ESV) *But the fruit of the Spirit is love, joy, peace, patience, kindness, goodness, faithfulness, gentleness, self-control; against such things there is no law.*

John 10:14 (NKJV) *I am the good shepherd; and I know My sheep, and am known by My own.*

Psalm 34: 8-10 (ESV) *Oh, taste and see that the Lord is good! Blessed is the man who takes refuge in him! Oh, fear the Lord, you his saints, for those who fear him have no lack! The young lions suffer want and hunger; but those who seek the Lord lack no good thing.*

# ABOUT THE AUTHOR

Marteka Landrum is originally from Topeka, Kansas. She attended college at Howard University, Washburn University, and Wichita State University where she graduated with a Bachelor of Arts in Education in 2001. In 2004, she received certification in English as a Second Language. In 2020, Marteka relocated to Northwest Arkansas. In 2021, she published her first book *Broken Warrior: Be Empowered to Overcome*.

Marteka enjoys helping others find their truth. She is a community builder who focuses on the individual. She has worked with various people groups and families across four continents, along with various counties across the United States. Marteka's gift is her voice and ability to reach others with her insight. Her purpose is to teach others how to be free. Through writing this book, Marteka hopes to let Christians know they can overcome past trauma, even after several years. Readers will be empowered to combat the lies, recognize who they were created to be, and have a strategy for moving forward. Marteka can be found on Instagram and Facebook @positive_changes11.

www.ingramcontent.com/pod-product-compliance
Lightning Source LLC
Chambersburg PA
CBHW072107110526
44590CB00018B/3345